KEEPING

AFRICAN CICHLIDS

COMPLETE BEGINNERS GUIDE ON KEEPING
AN AFRICAN CICHLID AQUARIUM

KEVIN MATOS

To get the best experience with this book, I've found readers also enjoy my book on Crystal Clear Aquarium Water which contains all the tips and tactics for having and keeping a beautiful-looking tank!

Available in eBook and Paperback

Purchase by visiting:

KaveManAquatics.com/crystal-clear-aquarium-water-ebook

Make sure to also visit KaveManAquatics.com for the best aquarium tips and advice!

Keeping African Cichlids is also available as an online video course.

If you are a visual and audio learner I highly recommend the course.

More information and details can be found at

KaveManAquatics.com/African-Cichlids-Course

For Yedenny, my inspiration to continue growing
and reaching our goals.
Thank you for you and our family!

TABLE OF CONTENTS

Introduction

We entered this hobby for a reason. To keep beautiful fish in a beautiful tank. Other reasons may include the bliss and peacefulness that keeping a fish tank brings. Digging deeper, we have an appreciation for beauty, art, and life. Whatever your reason is, you are not alone in this hobby!

I began this hobby as a kid, fascinated with my Goldfish in a bowl. But I was always under mom's roof so she was calling the shots on my wet pets. As an adult, I waited for the first piece of prime real estate to move in on my first big tank (A 20-gallon Octagon in a corner of my living room that surprisingly didn't have any furniture, lol)

Like many of us have learned, or will soon learn, this hobby grows on you quickly. My quantity of fish grew and so did my tank size. It grew to the point where my friends and family were amazed at what a beautiful fish tank looked like and they wanted one of their own. Naturally, they came to me for help and advice. Then the lockdown of 2020 happened and kept us all at home, and the only way to help my friends (visually) was by facetime and video. Que the birth of the YouTube Channel and here we are!

While everyone has their story and their reason for starting an aquarium, many of us are drawn to African Cichlids for the same reason. They are, after all, the most beautiful freshwater fish in the hobby, in my opinion anyway. But with anything beautiful, it ain't easy! If it were, everyone would keep African Cichlids. They are aggressive, and territorial and require specific water parameters. Things that many people, especially newcomers to the hobby would rather avoid dealing with. But I consider that a good thing because it keeps these fish unique to only those that truly want to take on the challenge for the reward of having a beautiful freshwater African Cichlid Tank.

BTW, I have great news for you. This book will show you how easy and simple it is! Then you can look like a total expert to your family and friends. By the end of this book, you'll be confident and comfortable with keeping these "Not for beginner" fish. Throughout the book, I'll be dropping plenty of helpful resources so you can take action when ready!

So, let's get on with learning everything you need to know about Keeping African Cichlids. Your beautiful tank is just around the corner! Let's Go!

Chapter 1

Introduction to African Cichlids

KAVEMAN AQUATICS

Lesson 1

BACKGROUND AND WHERE THEY COME FROM?

If you want to successfully keep African Cichlids then we must first learn a little about their origins, where they come from, and why they are such wonderful fish to keep. I promise this won't take long but we just need to start with a little history to understand these fish well. So where do they come from? Obviously, Africa right...

In the African Rift lakes, there are hundreds of different species, some haven't even been discovered yet. In the aquarium hobby, African Cichlids usually refer to the species found in the 3 main rift lakes that are in East Africa which are Lake Malawi, Lake Victoria, and Lake Tanganyika. All 3 of these lakes have different levels of salinity and water parameters so the species remain respective to their lakes.

Out of these 3 lakes, most African Cichlid keepers stick to the 700 or so different species that come from lake Malawi alone. The reason is that the lake Malawi species of fish are the most colorful of the 3 lakes.

The water conditions of lake Malawi and the other lakes is what makes keeping these fish a bit different than your typical tropical community tank. Lake Malawi consists of brackish water with a high pH range which simply means it's saltier than freshwater but not as salty as seawater. So African Cichlids kind of fit right in the middle, even though they are considered freshwater fish.

It's best to try and mimic the conditions of these lakes. Many African Cichlid keepers argue that these fish have been bought, bred, and sold in farms and stores for so long that they can live in a wide range of pH and water hardness. This is true, they can live and survive in a wide range, but if you follow my channel, you already know that I don't want my fish to survive, I want them to thrive! Later on, in the book, we'll discuss exactly how to achieve and maintain the best possible conditions for your African Cichlids.

The 3 main groups of fish in lake Malawi are Peacocks, Haplochromis, or Haps for short, and Mbuna. These groups have many different species among them with many different color pattern variations. There are so many to choose from including species that have cross-bred, you are sure to find many beautiful choices for your aquarium.

We'll get into specifics about each group later in the book.

Another big difference between these African Cichlids and your typical tropical aquarium fish is their aggression levels. These fish are very aggressive and this can become stressful for you, the fish keeper, if you don't know how to handle these aggression issues.

The reason for their aggression is very simple to explain, it's because of the ladies, lol seriously though, in an African Cichlid tank there is a hierarchy!

This hierarchy means that there is only 1 top dominant fish, also known as the tank boss, and then there's a number 2, number 3, and number 4, all in ranked order down to the bottom of the totem pole.

These fish will be aggressive towards each other to claim their position in that hierarchy and let me tell you, size does not matter, some little guys have more attitude than the bigger guys, it all depends on the species.

So, the closer they are to that top spot, the closer they are to mating with females. Only the most dominant male gets the females. It's the evolutionary story of survival of the fittest, and only the fittest get to mate.

The tank boss will be the fish that chases everyone around whenever he's in the mood too, he may even keep everyone on one side of the tank while he keeps the other side all to himself, I know very selfish....

But this is just a temporary show of force to let everyone know who's the boss. A good tank boss will occasionally pull this stunt, but it's not done with the intent to hurt anyone, only to reiterate his position.

A bad tank boss or a tank bully is trying to harm or kill other fish, this is no good and must be dealt with, we'll cover that later on in the book.

And the fish at the bottom of the hierarchy is also easily identified because he gets chased around by everyone else in the tank, still without the intent to harm, but this guy won't chase anyone around because there's no one below him in the ranks. Keep an eye on this guy and make sure he isn't too overly stressed.

But In order to successfully keep African Cichlids, there are methods to curb and mitigate this aggression that will keep you and your fish happy. We'll go over these methods in detail in the next lesson.

Lesson Outline:

- Most African Cichlids in the aquarium hobby come from Lake Malawi

- Be aware of the hierarchy

- Keep an eye on the fish at the bottom!

KAVEMAN AQUATICS

Lesson 2

DEALING WITH AGGRESSION

Dealing with aggression is going to be a very important skill to learn when keeping African Cichlids. The reason why we're discussing it so early in the book is that I don't want you to get discouraged by it.

This is one of the main reasons why these fish are not recommended to beginners but it's not that hard to deal with if you learn the techniques used by all African Cichlid keepers. And luckily, you're in good hands! I've had to learn the hard way what works and what doesn't. I've lost some of the most beautiful fish you've ever seen and had to re-home others. This is the part of the hobby beginners find discouraging if they can't get it right. But most of the time they can't get it right because they don't know how to, they've never done the research, and they've never been instructed. I've got you covered!

Let's talk about some methods of curbing the aggression in our African Cichlid tank.

A top technique in curbing some of the aggression in your tank is over-stocking. Yes, there's a reason why you've seen so many African tanks that are full of fish. It's not because the owners want to be mean and pack in as many fish as they can.

This tactic helps reduce aggression in the tank. Now don't get me wrong, this doesn't make an aggressive fish any less aggressive, what it does is it helps to mitigate that aggression on any one specific fish. Let me explain...

In an understocked tank the most aggressive fish, which will be the tank boss, will exert his aggression possibly on everyone. Or he may have a specific target that he likes to pick on the most. This poor fish will be heavily stressed out and could lead to disease and/or death. When you overstock a tank, that same aggressive fish may still show the same behavior but now his aggression is spread to more fish so that no one specific fish gets the brunt of his attacks. By spreading it around, it's minimized on each individual fish. So if you're having excessive aggression problems in your tank, the first thing you need to do is **add more fish.**

Another reason for aggression is defending territory. A good way to handle this is during water changes. When you add new, clean, nutrient-rich water to your tank, things kind of reset. This is a good time to move your décor around and reset their territory as well.

What happens is they have claimed a specific area of the tank and they want to defend their territory. It could be a specific rock they like or a cave they built or a hole in the substrate they dug out. By moving and changing décor around, you essentially reset the territories. You should also fill in any holes or hills that have been built, they love to do that. By resetting everything there's nothing to defend and you can get your guys to calm down. But just know it's a never-ending battle, they will rebuild and reclaim.

Another reason for aggression, going back to the underlying reason why these fish are aggressive to begin with, they want that top spot in the hierarchy for mating purposes. So when keeping African Cichlids in an aquarium, it is a great tactic to keep an all-male tank.

The reason is because of the constant battle to move up in the hierarchy, like we've already discussed, if there are any females in the tank, this battle will be amplified to a great extent.

Having females in the tank will have all the males fighting constantly to be more dominant than the next fish. Everyone will fight for the female's attention and you will never have peace in your tank. It's also common to have females in your tank and not even know it. Fish stores and breeders can easily get confused and sell you male fish that aren't all males. You could have a hidden female in the mix, especially if you're buying fish young, it's even harder to tell. Then you end up with a tank with constant fighting and splashing water and fish trying to kill each other and never understand why.... it's because of the females in your tank.

The only time you should have females is if you're specifically trying to breed. And in this case, you should have a separate breeder tank and there should be a ratio of about 5 females to every male.

So what if you're doing everything right, you're overstocking, no females in the tank, but you still have a bully? What do you do? Well, you remove him. Put him in quarantine alone for about 2 weeks. This will give the rest of the tank time to reset the hierarchy and then reintroduce him alone. Hopefully, a new tank boss will put him in his place and things will be fine but this doesn't work all the time. Sometimes the answer is just to re-home that bully.

In the next lesson, we'll talk about what fish can be mixed together and which you should avoid, especially just starting.

Lesson Outline:

- African Cichlid aggression is what labels them as "Not for beginners"

- Overstocking your tank is the best tactic, among others, for curbing aggression

- Keeping an all-male tank helps with aggression

- Remove a bully from your tank and rehome if you have to

Lesson 3

MIXING PEACOCKS AND HAPS

In lake Malawi there are 3 main groups of African Cichlids. Peacocks, Haplichromis (Haps), and Mbuna. We'll go over some similarities and differences and what would be the best combinations for a successful tank.

It's a common general rule of thumb that you don't want to mix all 3 in the same tank for various reasons that we'll go over. But with that being said, I also want to let you know that it has been done many times with success. But it's very challenging, especially for beginners, due to the different needs and temperaments of the groups.

So I would recommend that you stick with one of the groups I'll cover in this chapter for your best chances of success.

Peacocks and Haps are the most common mix for beginners just starting with African Cichlids. There are a few good reasons for this mix. Peacocks and Haps have similar diets, similar temperaments, and similar swimming styles, making them a good fit to mix with each other and get a nice color variety in your tank.

Peacocks and Haps are free swimmers so their aqua-scaping needs are similar. Usually, you'd add some small rocks or décor that take up space in the bottom 1/3 of the aquarium, allowing for plenty of swimming space in the middle and top 2/3's.

This will allow for some hiding spots when needed while not over-crowding your tank with décor and losing the swimming space they need.

Their diet is similar as they are both omnivores which means they eat both meat and veggies. A mixed feeding regiment of high proteins and veggies is best for both peas and haps.

Many options can be fed to these fish which also makes them enjoyable to watch as they munch on some homemade shrimp or some frozen Krill. We'll dive deeper into feeding your African Cichlids later.

Peacocks are the most colorful out of the 3 groups so many fish keepers are drawn to them, but keeping your tank stress free is important.

These African Cichlids can change their colors almost immediately when stressed or when submissive. Only the most dominant fish will display the brightest of colors while the submissive guys, lower down in the totem pole may dull their colors in an attempt to display them-selves as non-threatening to the dominant fish.

When a fish is being chased around and stressed out, its color may fade. But that same fish if placed in a separate tank on his own or with other submissive fish, making him the tank boss, can brighten his colors over-night!

Keep in mind as previously discussed, it's the males that show color, not females.

Adult Peacocks can grow to about 6" while some Haps can grow to about 10-12 inches or more. This is why researching the specific species you want is important. You wouldn't want to purchase a fish that grows to 12" while only having a 55-gallon tank. That fish will be stressed and most likely be very aggressive and territorial.

Peacocks are the least aggressive of the 3 groups, but keep in mind this doesn't mean they're not aggressive, just comparatively less than the other two.

Also, some species of Peacock can be very aggressive like Dragon bloods, or Eurika reds. But these are hit or miss, sometimes you get a nice one, and sometimes you can get a complete psycho...so trial and error.

Peacocks and Haps are generally the best mixes to start with when starting an African Cichlid tank. Their temperaments are a good starting point to get **you** accustomed to it and learn how to adjust and correct issues when they come up.

In the next lesson, we'll talk about having an Mbuna-only tank, another great option!

Lesson Outline:

- Peacocks and Haps can successfully be mixed together

- Peacocks and Haps are both Omnivores

- There are aggressive peacocks and peaceful peacocks, but overall, they are generally the most peaceful out of the 3 groups

KAveMAN AQUATICS

Lesson 4

MBUNA ONLY TANK

If you're drawn to the look and variety of Mbuna African Cichlids, then your best bet is to have an Mbuna-only tank.

Mbunas have a completely different personality and you will have a completely different tank experience keeping them.

With so many species of Mbuna, the color varieties you can have are endless and can result in a beautiful-looking tank.

Unlike Peacocks and Haps, some female Mbuna can show bright vibrant colors just like their male counterparts, but keep in mind that females will also increase the aggression in your tank if the ratios aren't correct.

Mbunas are very territorial and are the most aggressive of the 3 groups. When mixed with the other 2, Mbuna will drive the others nuts.

Especially if the Mbuna are of equal size, and even worse if they're bigger. This is why when deciding to keep Mbuna, it's best to keep them with each other to not stress out the other fish in your tank.

Yes, they will be aggressive with each other as well but they will be ready and accustomed to that type of aggression.

Mbuna differ from Peacocks and Haps in various ways.

For starters, they are rock dwellers, which means they love to dart in and out of rock crevices and hide and build caves to protect as their territory.

When aquascaping for an Mbuna tank it should be very rocky with caves and caverns.

You will enjoy the site of Mbuna popping in and out of cracks in your décor.

You can stack rocks on top of each other as well to break up the line of sight across the tank which aids in reducing aggression. It always helps when the bully can't find their target.

Limestone rock is very beneficial as it will also help in buffering your water and keeping PH high which they require. We'll discuss plenty about PH later.

Mbunas are herbivores that require a veggie-based diet. Keeping protein portions small in their diet is important as they are very susceptible to Malawi bloat which is a very common disease among African Cichlids.

They will also feed on algae in your tank that grows on the glass and décor.

Fasting your African Cichlids for 1 day a week helps in reducing the chance of bloat by allowing them extra time to digest and release.

Mbunas specifically do well with this 1 day fast as they'll go to the rocks and graze on them if they still want to snack.

We've already discussed overstocking as a means to curb aggression but this is especially helpful with Mbuna.

Mbuna will claim a piece of real estate and defend it to death. If any male seems like a threat, they will unleash the beast on them.

A good practice is to keep only 1 of any species as 2 or more of the same species will almost always fight to be the most dominant male.

Being that there aren't any females around to release themselves with, they will take their aggression out on each other and it won't be pretty.

Male Mbuna don't like being surrounded by other big bright beautiful males that want to take their territory. But it gets worse if there are females around. Especially if there are only 1 or 2 females that all the other 20-30 males want...That's a problem waiting to happen.

Remember with African Cichlids you always want a high female-to-male ratio to avoid aggression problems. But this should only be done when attempting to breed. Other than breeding, a male-only Mbuna tank is the way to go.

If you do choose to keep females, be prepared for fry as these fish will mate. More on breeding and fry later.

In the next lesson, we'll talk about some suitable tank mates for your African Cichlids to give you even more variety.

Lesson Outline:

- Mbuna should be kept in a Mbuna-only tank

- Mbuna are herbivores and require a veggie-based diet

- Too much protein can cause Malawi Bloat

- Mbuna are rock dwellers

KAVEMAN AQUATICS

Lesson 5

TANK MATES

When it comes to tank mates for your African Cichlids, the choices are going to be pretty slim. But that's ok, because the number 1 best tank mate for African Cichlids...is other African Cichlids. That's right!

And since they come in so many different species and colors, you can have a beautiful looking, full-of-color, African Cichlid tank.

As long as you stick to the previous suggestions of only keeping Peacocks and Haps together, or Mbuna together, especially if you're a beginner.

Depending on tank size you should always start with a minimum of about 5 or 6. Remember, having more fish mitigates the aggression imposed on any 1 fish. If you've got a bigger tank with more swimming space, you can start with more. Keep in mind that the more you add to the bio-load, the more your filtration will need to keep up.

But I won't leave you hanging like that, there are a few others known in the hobby to mix well with African Cichlids and they also serve some purpose in your tank.

The first one up is the clown loach! These guys are awesome-looking fish and they do a great job of sifting through your substrate looking for trapped food. That sifting will also free up any trapped detritus so that it can float away and find your filter intake!

Clown loaches do well in big groups of about 5-10 or more, but at least 5. If they are alone, they tend to just hide and never come out.

Clown loaches can grow to an enormous size, over 12" but they are slow growers. It will take them a long while to get that big. So get them small but big enough not to be targets for your African Cichlids.

Next up is the pleco! Plecos are great at controlling the algae build-up in your tank. They will clean your glass, décor, equipment...anything that algae can grow on, these suckers will get rid of it. The common pleco can also grow into a monster so I prefer the Bristle nose Pleco. This guy has bristles on his nose which he can also use to defend himself against aggressive African Cichlids and they only grow to about 5-6"

I can consider these 2, the bristle nose pleco and a group of clown loaches as my cleaning crew. They'll do a great job keeping your tank clean and add to the variety of fish in your tank.

Before moving on to the next lesson, let's touch on some other tank mates that you may come across when seeing other people's tanks. Some African Cichlid keepers also keep their guys with cichlids from other parts of the world, like American Cichlids.

American Cichlids are your Oscars, Jack Dempseys, Green Terrors, Blood Parrots, Red Devils, Severums...plenty to choose from.

So first I want to give you a technical explanation of why you shouldn't mix these fish. The most important reason is that the water they come from is very different. While we keep our African Cichlids in hard alkaline water with a high PH, American Cichlids are kept in softer acidic water with a lower PH. The difference in these waters can cause a fish to live a stressful life.

Another reason is their temperaments. Some African Cichlids can be too aggressive to live with Americans but that's not to say that an adult Oscar won't eat a juvenile African Cichlid, because it will.

But with that being said, I want to tell you that many in the hobby have broken these rules because honestly, they are flexible. If you can ensure that your fish has adjusted well to your water parameters and is not stressed from being bullied or tortured then it can be done, and it has been done in many tanks.

For true beginners, I would recommend that you don't do this mix...yet. Focus on establishing a healthy peaceful African Cichlid tank first before experimenting.

I keep a red Blood Parrot American Cichlid with my African Cichlids and he does just great at a PH of 8.0. Gordo is the OG of the tank. But keep in mind that something like this isn't guaranteed to work in your tank just because it worked in mine. Every tank is different.

In the next lesson, we'll cover a topic that many newcomers to the African Cichlid world are surprised to find out about, Plants....or the lack thereof.

Lesson Outline:

- A cleaning crew like plecos and clown loaches are great tank mates

- African Cichlids should be kept with other African Cichlids

- Mixing Africans and Americans can be done but isn't advised

Lesson 6

PLANTS, OR LACK THEREOF

Let's talk about plants, but before we do just know this will be a very short lesson. Why, because the consensus is that you can't keep plants with African Cichlids for a few reasons.

Most plants don't do well in the alkaline water that we keep our African Cichlids in, so that eliminates a bunch of choices right off the bat. Now for the plants that can survive in a high pH, there are still other problems. African Cichlids are diggers and sifters and love to move substrate around, most species will just uproot your plants and they'll eventually die.

But yes there are ways to bury those roots or put some heavy rocks around them so the fish can't uproot them. Well, for the plants that don't get uprooted the other problem is that they can be eaten. Most species will eat your plants, especially Mbuna that are herbivores, and love them some veggies!

For plants to thrive they also need a lot of light to grow and flourish, well a lot of light in an African Cichlid tank that most likely will always have a good level of nitrates and phosphates in it is going to create algae growth.

And you may be in a battle with algae in your African tank without plants already, so adding more potential algae growth isn't going to be fun.

And yes, there's a great effective way of combatting algae with a pleco right...yes very true, but do you know what else that pleco will LOVE to munch on...yea you guessed it, your plants!

All these reasons are why you hardly ever see live plants in an African Cichlid tank, but notice I said HARDLY.

With all that being said I'm not going to be the guy that says it can't be done...because it has been done, it's just super tricky to be successful at it.

But because it's super tricky and I've never actually wanted live plants in my tanks, I've never bothered to make the effort. But don't worry, I won't just leave you hanging like that.

A few plants that have the best chances of surviving with African Cichlids are Java fern, Anubias, and Vallisneria. These plants can do well in alkaline water and low levels of light. But you still have to figure out a way to ensure they don't get uprooted. Placing them in a potted, weighted holder may help.

If you're just setting up your tank, a good way is to plant the plants into your substrate and give them a few weeks to grow their roots and attach themselves well before adding in fish. This way when they do tug at them, and they will, it'll be harder to pull them out. Maybe they'll learn and stop trying after a while...maybe not.

Now if you wanted plants just for the benefits that plants provide to an aquarium, like reducing nitrate levels and keeping them low, consider a plant like Pothos which only needs its roots submerged in water.

With Pothos the leaves can grow above your aquarium with the roots in the water and most species of Africans will leave the roots alone. Be warned though, Pothos grows fast and large, you will need to trim.

If you have a sump for filtration, you can use a section as a refugium and keep live plants in there to get the nitrate-reducing benefits of plants.

Sorry if this lesson busted your bubble a bit, but the good news is that you've completed the first chapter! Congrats...in the next chapter we'll cover the equipment you need in the African Cichlid tank to ensure a clean, healthy, and peaceful tank!

Lesson Outline:

- Plants...good luck!

- Pothos works great above your tank with roots hanging in the water

- A sump is a great place for plants

Chapter 2

Equipment Matters

KAVEMAN AQUATICS

Lesson 7

TANK SIZES AND FISH NUMBERS

To get right to the point, you need to have a minimum of 55 gallons to keep African Cichlids...Now let me elaborate.

Keeping African Cichlids is unique, it's special, and it's different from keeping other fish. With a regular fish tank, mixed with your typical tropical aquarium fish, you'll have 1 or 2 of one species, like angel fish. 1 or 2 of another species say, tetras or something but when keeping African Cichlids, you've got a whole tank of African Cichlids. And not much else, if anything else is going to be in your tank.

This means you have to think of tank size for the entire stock you keep and not necessarily what 1 species of fish needs.

For example, an Oscar is an American Cichlid that gets huge fast, and that 1 Oscar fish requires a 75-gallon tank, by itself! 2 Oscars need about 125 gallons!

But with African Cichlids, yea if you had only 1 or 3, they will have plenty of space in a small tank.

But number 1, it's not just about the space.

And number 2, you probably won't be able to keep just 1 or 3....1 African Cichlid can't be mixed in with your community tank, it'll most likely kill everything else in there. If you did have a separate tank for 2 or 3 African Cichlids, they'd kill each other over dominance issues.

So the first reason why you need a minimum of 55 gallons is that African Cichlids are very active and love to swim, these are not boring fish. They need the swimming space. And when I say space, I don't mean up and down, I mean side to side. 55 gallons is the first tank size that comes in a 48" length. This is the true minimum. The 48" length. So always opt for a long tank over a tall tank.

Every tank owner wants to add their special touch by adding décor. While décor does add beneficial hiding spots and resting spots for your fish, it also takes up swimming space. An African Cichlid tank usually has a minimal amount of décor. Unless you're keeping Mbuna which like a lot of rocks to dart in and out of.

Also, they grow fairly quickly. In 1 year, your juveniles could reach adult size which could be anywhere from 6" to 12" depending on the species.

Then there's the big issue of aggression to deal with. Remember that the best way to curb aggression is to overstock your tank. You can't over stock a small tank, it will add to the stress of the fish already being in a confined space. By having a minimum of 55 gallons you can slightly overstock while still allowing them the swimming space they need.

Here are my recommendations for how many fish you can have max in your tank.

55 gallon tank = 15-20 Fish

65 gallon tank = 20-25 Fish

75 gallon tank = 25-30 Fish

125 gallon or more= 50+ You will lose count of how many you can keep.

Give or take a few obviously...these numbers aren't set in stone.

Remember that these are overstocked tanks so you will need to over-filtrate as well. But we'll get into that in the next lesson.

Now that I've beaten the horse about the minimum tank size, let me make a recommendation for you...

These fish are beautiful! And as you progress in your African Cichlid keeping, you will find even more beautiful species. You're going to want every gorgeous fish you see in your tank, don't worry, this is all normal behavior...especially for new guys lol

But as you add more and more fish to your tank, you could start pushing the limits of overstocking and you'll begin to feel like they need more space, meaning a bigger tank.

I guarantee you'll get this feeling while keeping these fish, you'll want a bigger tank not only to give your guys more space but also to add more guys! Lol

So my advice is this...Don't take the safe route and start small...I think you should start with the biggest tank your budget and your space allow for right now!

I know you may worry about if you're going to stick with the hobby, or if you're going to keep up with the work required.

Number 1, if you bought this book, I'm pretty sure you're into fish keeping and love these fish.

And number 2 if you don't stick with it there is a HUGE market out there for used aquarium equipment. You will have no problem selling your used tank and filters, someone will gladly take it off your hands…at a fraction of what you paid for everything of course.

But I doubt that's gonna be the case! You're going to get years of enjoyment out of your tank, especially with African Cichlids. So go ahead and get that big beautiful tank now, and you can thank me later ☺

Now with a big beautiful overstocked African Cichlid tank, it's going to require some heavy filtration. Let's get into that in the next lesson.

Lesson Outline:

- 55 Gallon Minimum Tank Size

- African Cichlids are very active and love to swim

- Get the biggest tank your space and budget allow for now

Lesson 8

OVER FILTRATION

With a heavily stocked African Cichlid tank comes a heavy bio-load. When these fish reach adult size you can expect to see some *rocks* floating around and hanging out on your substrate. The poop is real!

We have to combat this with some heavy filtration. More than what's usually recommended for your tank size. Filter manufacturers aren't taking into account that not only do you have fish that poop heavy and often, but you've got a bunch of them all in one tank!

So don't rely on the filter manufacturer's recommended tank size. I suggest that you double up on the specs….let me give you an example.

Let's say you've got a 55-gallon and are looking at a Hang on Back filter, or HOB for short, which if you're a beginner is a good choice of filter, to begin with.

So you choose to go with a Marine Land penguin 350 which the manufacturer says filters 50 -75 gallons per hour.

You might think that would be good enough but the manufacturer doesn't know you're keeping African Cichlids. So my suggestion would be to double up, and get 2 of these HOBs and that will give you the filtration you need to keep the water crystal clear and also ensure there's enough beneficial bacteria to remove all the harmful toxins from your water.

If you don't want 2 HOBs on your tank then go with one that's rated at 110 GPH or more...you get the point.

Now one more example if you were to choose to go with a canister filter. With canister filters, it's a bit different. I wouldn't ever go with the manufacturer's recommended size of aquarium. The marketing is kind of misleading...

They get that recommended aquarium size based on the filter's flow rate. But that flow rate is usually determined with an empty canister, with no media at all inside. But who runs a canister without media? Nobody!

Once you add all your media, sponges, bio-media, and chemical media, it will drastically reduce the manufacturer's stated flow rate.

To keep it simple, I've learned to take that advertised aquarium size and simply cut it in half.

If you've got a 90-gallon tank and see a Fluval 407 canister filter that's rated for up to a 100-gallon tank, simply cut that in half! Either get 2 Fluval 407s or get a canister that's rated for a 200-gallon tank.

For an African Cichlid tank specifically, I recommend turning your tank over about 8-10X per hour. Depending on the size and quantity of fish. If you have a 100 Gallon tank, your filtration flow rate should be:

$100 \times 8 = 800$ GPH

or

100 x10 = 1,000 Gallons/hour (keeping in mind not to use the manu-facturers stated flow rate! You'll want to cut that in half)

These rates can vary based on your maintenance practices as well.

Not only will your fish be happier and healthier with much cleaner water, but you also get to enjoy the beauty of a crystal-clear tank.

In the next lesson, we'll wrap up the required equipment with more of a recommended piece of equipment.

Lesson Outline:

- Over-filtrate your African Cichlid Tank

- Cut the manufacturers stated recommended tank size for any filter in half

- Turn tank over 8-10x per hour

KAVEMAN AQUATICS

Lesson 9

WATER MOVEMENT & CURRENT

Another very important piece of equipment in your African Cichlid tank is a wave maker or a power head.

Wavemakers are usually found in reef tanks providing the current and flow that corals need to grow and thrive. But it's very beneficial in a freshwater tank as well, especially with African Cichlids.

These fish are very active and love to swim! Providing them with more flow and current has multiple benefits.

One is, it will help curb aggression. If your guys are busy playing in the current, releasing some pent-up energy swimming against the flow, they'll spend less time thinking about each other, less time focused on protecting territory.

Think about your guys just floating around in still water, oh they're going to find a way to release some energy!

It's an added measure that can help reduce the aggression in your tank, even if it's just a small decrease in your particular tank, it's worth it!

Another great reason for a wave maker is it helps in keeping your tank clean! These active, large, hungry fish can produce a lot of waste. Waste that can accumulate in your tank between cleanings.

All that poop hanging out in your tank is going to contribute to a cloudy-looking tank and nobody wants that!

By adding a wavemaker and placing it in the right position, you can create a constant vortex of motion in your tank.

This will help in eliminating those dead spots where waste and uneaten food and debris can accumulate. It will keep it all moving until it eventually finds your filter intakes and that'll get it out of your tank.

Positioning your wavemaker as it relates to your filter intake and output is very important to achieve this circular water movement in your tank.

In short, you should place your wave maker close to the surface of your tank, angled upwards toward the surface, and on the same side as your filter intake.

If you want a more detailed explanation of the proper placement of a wavemaker, I have a great video tutorial on YouTube. Simply search "Kaveman Wavemaker".

The reason why you want it near the surface and angled upwards is to create surface agitation, which leads me to the next benefit of a wavemaker.

Because African Cichlids are very active, grow fast and live in high-temperature waters, they have a fairly high metabolism rate.

This means that they require a lot of oxygen. And if you're overstocking your tank as you probably should be, you'll need that much more oxygen in your tank.

For those of you that don't know this, it's the breaking of the surface tension that releases CO2 from your water and adds oxygen into your water.

We'll go deeper into the importance of adequate oxygen levels later in the book.

So make sure you add that wave maker, or 2 if you started with a tank of about 75 gallons or more. You'll see much clearer and cleaner water, and your fish will be happier and healthier.

To wrap up this chapter on required equipment I want to also mention the obvious for those very, very, new guys....

You also need a heater rated for your tank size as these fish require higher than usual temps to thrive.

More on required temps in the next chapter.

And you also need a light for your tank. Not because your fish need any light, they don't, natural light is more than enough for them, but I'm sure you'd like to see your fish at night so also make sure you get yourself a decent tank light rated for your size aquarium.

If you choose not to run a wavemaker in your tank, which is fine, to each their own, you will need some source of aeration, as I said these guys require a heavily oxygenated tank.

Make sure you get an air pump attached to an airstone big enough to provide enough bubbles in your tank to adequately break up the surface allowing for the transfer of oxygen into your tank.

In the next lesson, we'll go over some very important water parameters specifically for your African Cichlids as well as some safety measures to put in place that'll help you and your fish sleep well at night.

Lesson Outline:

- Adding a Wavemaker is very beneficial in an African Cichlid tank

- Wavemakers help keep your tank clean

- Without a wavemaker ensure you have adequate surface agitation

Chapter 3

Maintaining Optimal Water Parameters

KAVeMAN AQUATICS

Lesson 10

PH MATTERS

Some of you may think of PH or water hardness and feel like it's not that important. But your water's PH level is probably the number 1 biggest difference between keeping regular tropical community fish and keeping African Cichlids. (Successfully)

This is another one of the top reasons why these fish are categorized as not for beginners because you've got to mess with your water's chemistry.

Normally you could probably keep 95% of all the fish in your local fish store directly in your regular tap water (dechlorinated tap water of course).

But not African Cichlids.

Now explaining what PH is and how and why it fluctuates is a huge task that can be very confusing!

There are plenty of videos on YouTube **trying** to explain it thoroughly but good luck with those.

This book is about African Cichlids so I'm going to give you some of the specific details you need to understand in order to keep these fish.

PH ranges from 0-14 with 7.0 being neutral. Anything below 7.0 is considered acidic and anything above 7.0 is considered alkaline.

African Cichlids prefer a PH range between 7.5-8.4

First thing you need to do is test your tap water for PH.

If you don't have an API master test kit, then get one because you're gonna need it. It is an essential tool in this hobby in general, not just for African Cichlids.

You can find all the products and equipment discussed in this book here – KaveManAquatics.com/Shop

If you're lucky and your tap water is already alkaline, meaning above 7.0, then you may not even have to worry about adjusting your PH. If you're at even the low range of 7.5, I would suggest leaving it alone.

PH can become a difficult issue when you have to adjust it. Sometimes adjusting it and chasing a specific PH range can do more harm than good to your fish.

These fish can adjust to the PH range they're in but it's the swings and changes in PH that do damage. What you want to try to achieve is keeping your PH constant and steady. Don't worry, I'm going to show you how.

But again, if your tap water is at about 7.5 then you're good! Leave it alone, your fish will be fine, move on to the next lesson...no, I'm just kidding, this will still be good info for you.

Now for the rest of us that have acidic tap water, meaning below 7.0, then we have to raise our PH to keep African Cichlids. There are a few ways to do that.

1ˢᵗ way involves adding products to your water. But this isn't the most efficient way. Seachem Cichlid Lake Salt and Malawi buffer both work great at raising and maintaining your pH levels as well as making your water harder by adding the proper dosage during every water change. But you have to stay consistent.

Salt does not evaporate with your water but your buffer will get used up as the nitrates in your tank build up making your water more acidic, lowering your PH. The buffer is what fights back as your water becomes acidic and maintains your higher PH levels.

When you replace water that has no salt or buffer, you have to consistently add the required dosage to the volume of the new water being introduced. This takes dedication and precision but also takes a toll on your pockets, eventually, every time you need to re-up on these products.

An alternative is to use a natural source like Crushed Coral or Aragonite Sand.

Crushed Coral and Aragonite sand both release minerals into your water that provides the buffer required to raise and stabilize your PH.

With Crushed Coral, you have a choice of either adding it into your filter so water will be passing directly through it, or you can add it to your current substrate. Aragonite Sand is too fine to add in a filter but it can be used with your substrate.

While both of these work great at raising and maintaining your PH, they too will eventually lose their buffering capacity. But it can take years before the need to replace substrate and months before the need to replace the crushed coral in your filter.

Again, this is the part of keeping African Cichlids that can seem confusing and intimidating...but it's not.

I keep my PH right around 8.0. I mix crushed coral and aragonite sand into my substrate and I also add Cichlid Lake Salt during every water change to maintain water hardness. This ensures my water always has a good amount of buffering capacity to keep my PH stable, which is the priority.

I test my PH level before a water change at the end of the week. If the levels are lower than they typically are, I don't add *more* lake salt and/or Malawi buffer. That would be chasing the pH and not the right thing to do.

Instead, this is an indication that my crushed coral and/or aragonite sand is losing its buffering capacity and it may be time to replace some or all of it.

By consistently testing and monitoring your water's PH you will get a feel of when it's time to replace your coral and/or aragonite sand.

Hopefully, you've got a good grasp of where your PH needs to be and how to get it there. In the next lesson, we'll discuss the water temperature required for your African Cichlids and some very important safety measures.

Lesson Outline:

- African Cichlids thrive in their proper pH range from 7.5-8.4

- Swings in your pH are stressful to your fish. Keeping PH stable is the priority

- Use a natural source for buffering water like crushed coral or aragonite sand. When that's not an option Seachem Cichlid Lake Salt and Malawi Buffer will get the job done

KAVeMAN AQUATICS

Lesson 11

TEMPERATURE REQUIREMENTS

African Cichlids have a specific temperature range that's different from most tropical fish. They prefer their water a bit warmer in the range of 78-82 degrees.

Keep in mind that at these temps their behavior will be noticeably different. The higher the temp, the faster their metabolism. They'll be more active, they'll be hungrier, and they'll need to eat more. This will also make them more aggressive. Hungry fish take their frustration out on each other.

I've had my temp set at 82 and noticed the increase in activity. Feeding them a bit more may have calmed them down but I would be sacrificing water quality as that extra food has to come out the other end too.

I changed my setup and decided that an even 80 degrees keeps most of the aggression to a minimum and I can continue to feed the normal amount. We'll get into the quantity and frequency of feedings a bit later in the course.

Now it's as simple as setting your desired temp on your heater and this lesson would be over. But I wanted to give you some extra helpful info on temperature and heaters.

These fish are expensive, and if you're overstocking, the dollars can add up. Well, accidents happen! And electrical equipment can sometimes fail. Trust me when I say I've seen it happen, multiple times.

A heater can fail you in 2 ways, 1 it stops working, it just goes dead...little do you know your tank's temp has been dropping hour after hour until eventually, you walk up to a tank full of dead fish!

2, the temp sensor fails and stays stuck in the on position. In this nightmare scenario, you can come home to your fish all over the floor...because they tried to save themselves from being cooked alive only to suffocate on the floor instead.

This is a heartbreaking sight on so many levels and I hope you never have to see this with your own eyes.

So I want to help you with a very simple safety measure you can put in place tomorrow and prevent this from happening to you and your fish.

It's simply called redundancy. By having 2 redundant heaters set up you can cut down on the chances of something like this happening. Let me explain.

Even though one heater is sufficient to heat your tank, you should have 2. Using a 100-gallon tank as an example, 1 heater at (300w) is sufficient for 100 gallons. Instead of getting 1 (300 w) that can heat (100 gallons), get 2 (200w). The 2 (200w) heaters will work together to reach the desired temp. What does this accomplish you ask, good question.

In one of the scenarios mentioned earlier, a heater can be stuck in the on position. With this redundant heating system, if one heater gets stuck in the "on" position, it won't be powerful enough to severely overheat your tank. The other heater, simply won't turn on at all. This can buy you time to recognize that one heater is malfunctioning and correct the problem.

The other scenario was that 1 heater stopped working completely, well with a redundant system the other functioning heater will just be working harder to achieve the desired setting, keeping temps as close as possible to the tank water's temp. Again, buying you some time to recognize the problem and correct it.

This safety measure alone can save your fish someday! And I'd rather have it and never need it than need it and not have it.

In the next lesson, we'll discuss aerating your tank and why it's important, and of course, I'll have another easy safety measure you can put in place because it's all about keeping your guys safe!

Lesson Outline:

- Keep the Temperature stable at about 78-82 degrees

- Use a redundant safety measure to prevent any accidental equipment failures that can be deadly

KAVEMAN AQUATICS

Lesson 12

OXYGEN LEVELS

Oxygen in any aquarium with any type of fish is important. Every aquarist should know how to properly aerate their tank. Either by use of bubblers, air stones, or wavemakers. This is one of the must-haves or must-knows when keeping fish.

But when keeping African Cichlids, it's critical! For multiple reasons. As we already discussed in the previous chapter, the higher-than-normal temps these fish require, and their high activity levels is what give these guys a very fast metabolism rate. Which results in consuming a lot of oxygen in the water.

Now, that's only referring to them individually. When it comes to your tank as a whole, we know that most likely you'll be overstocking your tank to help with aggression. Having an overstocked tank of fish in which each one is already consuming high levels of oxygen.... well, that should be a clear sign of how much oxygen you need in an African Cichlid tank.

But that's easy to achieve, add some airstones, add strong wavemakers, you'll have a good amount of surface agitation and your tank will be well oxygenated.

But because we're keeping African Cichlids, and because oxygenation is that much more important for us, I wanted this lesson to be more about backing up your oxygen in case of an emergency.

If for whatever reason you were to lose power to your tank, and all your air pumps and wavemakers turned off, it will always be a lack of oxygen that kills your fish first.

In an overstocked African Cichlid tank, if the power goes out, the oxygen in that water will be gone in no time.

So let's be prepared if this situation were to ever happen.

First, a worst-case scenario you weren't prepared at all…and now the power is out. Grab a big cup or 2 and dunk it in the water and then pour the water back into the tank. Do this continuously with a few short breaks in between until power comes back or until you can install a battery-operated air pump.

Second, in the best-case scenario, be prepared with a battery-operated air pump already installed on your tank for just such an emergency.

This battery-operated pump should not be your primary air pump. Make sure the batteries are new and have charge and keep an air stone in your tank attached to this backup source.

I use the PennPlax SB11 which monitors the power at the outlet. If it senses a power outage, it automatically kicks itself on using the batteries to provide oxygen to your tank.

(KaveManAquatics.com/Shop)

This is especially helpful if the power outage were to happen while no one was home. Without this backup, during a power outage, with no one home to do the first method we discussed, you will come home to an entire tank of dead fish. I've seen it happen. Don't let this be you.

Not only are these very expensive fish, but once you get to know them and their personalities, you will develop an attachment to them and it can be heartbreaking if something like this were to happen.

I've seen some people leave the hobby entirely after a disaster like this, don't let it happen to you, be prepared!

The water parameters discussed in this chapter for PH levels, temperature, and oxygenation are specifically for African Cichlids.

But keep in mind that we still need to maintain the proper water parameters for all fish in general. Meaning our water should never have any ammonia or nitrite in it. And we should always try to keep a low level of nitrates. This is known as the nitrogen cycle. If you are very new to the hobby and don't know about this cycle you can refer back to my channel and watch the "Aquarium Beginners Start Here" playlist.

In the next module, we'll discuss how to maintain our African Cichlid tanks as well as how to care for our beautiful fish.

Lesson Outline:

- Higher temperatures require additional oxygenation

- Back up your oxygen source in case of power outages

- If not prepared for a power outage, dunking a cup in and out of your tank, and splashing the water back in can buy you some time.

Chapter 4

Care and Health

KAVEMAN AQUATICS

Lesson 13

FEEDING

We've got all the equipment we need, our water parameters are in check, and we've chosen the type of African Cichlid we'd like to keep.

In this chapter, we're going to discuss actually "keeping African Cichlids". How to care for them and make sure they are growing and staying healthy, and preventing and treating some common diseases.

If I took a wild guess at why you've chosen to keep African Cichlids, I'm going to get on a limb here and say it's because of their beautiful colors and patterns. Am I right? And you want to know how to bring out those colors as much as possible right?

Well unfortunately the best way to get the most color from your fish is their genetics and we can't do anything about that except find a good breeder. But besides good genetics, there are a few things we can do to help bring that beautiful color out in our fish and we're going to begin with their diet.

Their nutrition and diet are a major contributing factor to your fish's longevity, growth, health, and yes, their color. I am going to provide you guys with exactly what I feed, how I feed, and why, to get these beautiful colors out of my fish so you can achieve the same for your fish.

Some of you may have already seen my video on YouTube with information on the food and supplements I use but for this book, I'm going to cover everything that I feed to give you more options to choose from when it comes to supplementing their nutrition.

Before we begin, I just want to say that I am not endorsed or sponsored by any of these products, yet... They have not paid me to recommend them, even though I think they should lol. These are just my choice of products that through years of testing and experimenting I've found to work wonders for my fish and I know they will do the same for yours.

Also, by no means am I saying these are the best products out there, there may be something better, but I know these products I'm going to share with you will help you accomplish your goals of having beautiful, healthy, brightly colored fish!

The choice of food type is always going to be a pellet rather than any flakes. Flakes have much less nutritional value than any pellet will have. Flakes will also cause your water to cloud much more rapidly than a pellet would.

My pellet of choice has always been Northfin Cichlid food. I use all 3 formulas and mix them up throughout the week to give my guys some variation.

I use the regular Cichlid formula, the veggie formula, and the krill formula.

If you wanted to keep an Mbuna-only tank then I would only feed the veggie formula. This is part of the reason why it's very challenging to keep all 3 types together because your Mbuna should not eat the same amount of protein that your Peacocks and Haps should.

Northfin has proven to be a very high-quality food when it comes to nutrition and also tank water quality. But as good as Northfin is, it has a major problem, a problem that all commercial fish foods have.

During the production of these commercial fish foods, many nutrients are lost during the heating and drying process. It's just unavoidable. For that reason, I supplement my food with products that will enhance the food and complete the essential nutrients your fish need.

I supplement with GarlicGuard, Vitachem, Nourish, and ZooPlankton. All of which can be found at KaveManAquatics.com/Shop

Let's go through each one.

The first product is GarlicGuard from Seachem. Now most of us that have been in the hobby for a while already know about GarlicGuard and know that it's a flavor enhancer for fish, and it can get fish that don't want to eat, to eat. But there's more to GarlicGuard than that. Garlic contains Allicin which has a huge impact on fish health. Especially when it comes to disease and parasite resistance. I make sure I never run out of GarlicGuard and never miss a feeding without it. You can also use pure crushed garlic and get the same benefits. I add 1 capful of Garlic Guard to my pellets.

The next supplement is Nourish, also by Seachem. A very important vitamin that gets destroyed during commercial fish food processing is Vitamin C. Vitamin C is by far the most important vitamin for your fish. It helps your fish recover from illness as well as body and fin damage. You will notice amazing regrowth of fins damaged by fighting and aggression problems in your tank by adding this supplement daily. Nourish also contains Iodide which is a very important element to freshwater fish. I add 1 capful of Nourish to my pellets.

My next supplement is called Vitachem by Boyd Enterprises. Northfin food has a great number of amino acids but is missing some important ones. Vitachem is a multivitamin like we would take a multivitamin for ourselves every day. And it has many of the amino acids missing from commercial pellet foods. These amino acids will ensure healthy fish overall and also helps in fin regrowth as well. Vitachem is super concentrated at 1 drop per gallon of tank water. So I add about 10 drops to my pellets.

The last supplement I use is called ZooPlankton by Seachem. Zooplankton is essentially used in saltwater reef tanks to aid in coral growth and coloration. But ZooPlankton also provides a boost in natural melanin production which bring out the awesome color of fish that have high pigmentation...In other words, it'll help get your African Cichlids' color to pop!

Now let's put it all together. When feeding pellets, the key to not overfeeding is to make sure all the food is gone in about 1 minute or less. Any longer than that and you'll have problems that come with overfeeding like cloudy water and excessive fish waste.

I have about 50 fish in my 210 and I already know how much food I can serve that will get eaten in that time frame. For me, using the 3MM Northfin pellets, I feed 1.5 tablespoons. No, I don't measure it to an exact amount, I just eyeball it, I've pretty much gotten used to it.

Mix these supplements together with your desired pellets. Doesn't matter what order you add them in.

Quick recap. 1 capful of GarlicGuard, 1 capful of Nourish, 1 capful of ZooPlankton, and about 10 drops of the Vitachem which is very concentrated.

Once you got your concoction mixed up let it sit for 15-20 minutes to ensure the pellets soak up the entire mixture.

You'll know when it's ready for feeding time when almost all the liquid is gone. That means the pellets have soaked up all these nutrients and when the fish eat, they'll each get a direct shot of all the goodness!

Yes, you will get a short cloudiness from all the products added but not to worry, your water will clear back up in no time.

Now let's talk about feeding frequency. Believe it or not, these big African Cichlids don't need to eat much, just like most other fish. Since most of my fish are at full-grown adult size, I only feed them once a day and I fast them on Sundays.

Fasting them one day a week helps to clear out their digestive system and avoid any problems like Malawi bloat or swim bladder disease. It also helps to give your beneficial bacteria a short break from the ammonia accumulation and gives it time to catch up if needed.

Throughout the week, I change up their pellet feeding and mix in some other high-quality high-nutritional treats!

African Cichlids love Shrimp and Krill. So I surprise them on any random day of the week with Frozen shrimp. I use the frozen shrimp from Omega which has nothing but shrimp in it.

If your fish are juveniles, you can feed it to them as a whole frozen cube. They'll all pick at it and pull it apart slowly and everyone will get a good fill of it.

If you have bigger fish like mine that can swallow the whole cube, they will! In this case, what I do is add the cubes to a cup of tank water and let it thaw out for about 5 minutes and then add it to the tank. This will allow the shrimp to spread out so everyone can share the treat.

Side note, I don't ever turn off my filter when feeding pellets. There's no need to because they sink to the bottom and they're all gone before you know it.

But when feeding thawed-out frozen shrimp, I do turn them off. The small pieces of shrimp will find their way into your intake and then it's just a waste of food contributing to your bio-load.

Another great treat I like to feed is freeze-dried jumbo krill! This is a great source of vitamin E which will help their growth and they love this stuff.

My method of feeding the jumbo krill starts with turning off the filters as well for the same reason as the frozen shrimp.

I take my feeding portion, which for my guys is 2 heaping tablespoons. Because the jumbo krill is pretty jumbo, my smaller guys have trouble keeping an entire piece in their mouth and they eventually end up spitting it out. For them, I chop up 1 of the 2 tablespoons into about ¼ size pieces.

I'll serve the whole pieces first and all the big guys will scarf them down. Wait a few seconds and then serve the chopped pieces so the little guys get their fill as well.

One thing I will tell you is that this method can get very messy. There will be pieces of krill everywhere. For that I reason I tend to feed this the day before or even the day of a scheduled water change. Just to make sure any uneaten pieces don't stay in the tank.

Now don't worry, I didn't forget about you Mbuna guys. For Mbuna, in addition to the Northfin Veggie formula you can throw in a fresh vegetable like zucchini, pumpkin, or cucumber and they will tear it up.

These pieces of veggies will float so a cool method is to stick a fork in them and the fork will sink to the bottom with the veggies attached.

And yes, since Peacocks and Haps are omnivores, you could also try this treat for them as well.

Feeding your fish good quality high nutritional foods will not only boost their color and help them to grow, but it will strengthen your fish's immune system and help fend off diseases. It will ensure they live a long, happy, and healthy life so that you and your fish have many years of bonding time together!

In the next lesson, we'll discuss how water changing and keeping your tank clean will help boost your fish color as well as some specific African Cichlid products in our tanks to ensure our fish are thriving!

Lesson Outline:

- Your African Cichlid' diet is an essential part of their growth and color

- All mass-produced commercial foods lose essential nutrients during the heating and drying process

- Supplementing your food can provide more nutrients enhancing their life longevity and color

KaveMan Aquatics

Lesson 14

WATER CHANGING, CLEANING, AND VACUUMING

Water changes are a very important part of the aquarium hobby, and they are especially beneficial when keeping African Cichlids. I'll explain that in more detail in just a minute.

But first, let me speak on water changes in general.

There are always different levels of aquarium hobbyists. It's not just beginner and experienced. There are many levels in between. Some of this information may be very basic to you but I like to keep the beginner in mind that may be reading this book.

So very quickly I wanted to touch on the importance of water changes for the brand-new guys that need some catching up. And remember, we were all new to the hobby at some point.

Water changes are necessary for multiple reasons. One of them is because of the accumulation of nitrates in your tank. Nitrates are a harmful bi-product of the nitrogen cycle and the only way to remove them from your tank is with water changes.

I can't go into details on the nitrogen cycle here. That would be a whole course in itself, but if you don't know what the nitrogen cycle is I have a great video on YouTube explaining it in the simplest terms. Search YouTube for "Kaveman Nitrogen Cycle"

Live Plants will also help reduce your nitrates levels but as already previously discussed, we African Cichlid keepers don't really have that option. But even if we did, live plants wouldn't replace the need for water changes, it would just reduce it.

Another important reason for water changes is to re-introduce essential vitamins and minerals that have been used up by your fish in your current tank water. Adding new freshwater will replenish these minerals that your fish need to grow and stay healthy.

If you'd like more general information on why and how to do proper water changes again, I'll refer you back to my channel, plenty of helpful videos there.

In this lesson, I wanted to touch on the importance of these water changes when keeping African Cichlids.

As previously mentioned, an African Cichlid tank is usually heavily stocked. Because of this heavy stock, and also not being able to keep many live plants, if any at all, our nitrate levels will rise quickly.

An African Cichlid tank can easily pass 40PPM of nitrates in less than a week and maybe even reach 80PPM. These fish grow quickly and create a lot of waste, and the fact that you'll have so many in 1 tank will make those nitrates reach harmful levels quickly.

So with that being said, be prepared to do big, frequent, water changes. I do 80% weekly water changes and I suggest that you do no less than a 50% water change every week.

This will remove a major amount of the nitrates in your tank, but it's also very beneficial for your fish. Having this fresh clean water will help them grow and help their digestive systems to avoid diseases like Malawi bloat and swim bladder. But it also helps prevent all diseases in general. Also clean, fresh and mineral-rich water will make their colors pop!

Along with water changes you're going to want to make sure you keep your substrate clean and clear of any detritus. Detritus accumulation is only going to increase the already elevated levels of nitrates in your tank.

Using a wavemaker as previously discussed will be a major help in removing waste and uneaten food from any dead spots in your tank. One of the many great reasons to have a wave maker or 2 in an African Cichlid tank.

But even with a wavemaker, I still go in there every 2-3 weeks for a full deep substrate clean. I make sure to remove all the décor, which in my case isn't much, and make sure to vacuum all of the substrate for any detritus that may have been trapped under the décor.

Again, If you are new to the hobby and need help with how to vacuum your substrate, refer back to my channel. I want to keep this book specifically on African Cichlids for the more experienced aquarist that is already aware of general maintenance practices like substrate vacuuming.

Now, something we need to keep in mind because we're doing these big and frequent water changes is keeping the PH stable for our guys.

Using Cichlid Salt and Malawi buffer will both help in stabilizing PH. But if you don't already have a buffer in your tank, like aragonite sand or crushed coral as your substrate, there will be a fluctuation in the pH, and we already know that isn't good.

2 options.

You could pre-treat your new water. Add your Cichlid Salt and Malawi Buffer to a bucket or buckets of the new water you're going to use. After a few days, the pH will adjust according to your dosage levels and then you can add it to the tank. Keep in mind that this water needs to be heated to the tank water's old temp as well.

But I'm pretty sure to most of you that option doesn't sound too appealing.

The second option is to use aragonite sand or crushed coral or both as your substrate. This will always provide a constant source of buffer for your water. So when adding in new water, it will not alter the PH, or just slightly if it does. Then go ahead and add in your Malawi buffer which will assist in keeping your water stable with very minimal fluctuation.

Keep in mind that you want to add the same amount of Malawi buffer every water change, stay consistent so that you won't need to chase the PH because one week it was lower or higher than the next week. Remove the same amount of water and add the same amount of Malawi Buffer for each water change.

When it comes to your Cichlid salt, you only want to dose for the amount of the new water being added. Not the entire volume of your tank. This is very important.

As water evaporates, the salt does not. So whatever amount of salt you added previously remains in your tank.

As discussed previously, with your first-time setup, dose the salt for the entire tank's volume. After that only dose salt for the volume of new water being added.

Keep in mind that the products being recommended here are based on a source water that is too acidic for African Cichlids. These products are being added in order to raise the PH and harden the water.

If your source water is already hard and alkaline all of this can be avoided. Knowing your source water and how it needs to be manipulated, if at all, is important.

Another great product that I use during every water change and I recommend you do as well is Cichlid Trace. Cichlid trace has all the elements found in the African Rift lakes where these fish are found.

And no matter how long these fish have been away from their natural habitat, no matter how long they've been raised by a local breeder in a fish tank, that doesn't change hundreds of years of genetics and evolution. These fish need what they need, and if you know me you know that I don't want my fish to just survive, I want them to thrive!

Cichlid Trace and Cichlid Lake Salt have many of the same elements but what one is missing is found in the other. So I give my boys the best of both.

This last product will be obvious to most of you but it just can't go unsaid. Seachem Prime or Safe are an absolute must during every water change. But never to be used together!

You must always de-chlorinate your tap water! There, I said it lol.

But here's a tip I'm realizing many people aren't aware of. You don't need to dechlorinate the water in a separate bucket and then add it to your tank.

De-chlorinators are safe for your fish and work extremely fast. You can go ahead and add your de-chlorinator straight into your tank, just before adding in the new tap water.

Hopefully, you understand how important big and frequent water changes are when keeping African Cichlids. Keep up with your maintenance and watch your fish thrive!

In the next lesson, I'm going to show you how to distinguish between male and female African Cichlids. There are some signs to look for that are somewhat accurate but venting your fish is the only 100% accurate way.

Lesson Outline:

- An African Cichlid tank is going to require more maintenance than your average aquarium

- Big, frequent water changes will be necessary in order to keep high nitrate levels down to a safe amount

- Always dechlorinate your source water, even if you think there's no chlorine in your source

Lesson 15

VENTING AND SEXING

Since we already know that the best chance for success in your African Cichlid tank is to keep an all-male tank, it'd be a pretty good idea to learn how to tell the difference between males and females.

Some characteristics could help you "guess" but they aren't 100% accurate and then there's venting your fish which is 100% accurate. Let's cover both.

With Peacocks and Haps, most males show a lot of colors. They do this to look more dominant and attract females. This is why your tank boss is usually the brightest and most colorful. Most female Peacocks and Haps are washed out and are kind of a dull gray and don't show much color. Mbuna females on the other hand can show just as much color as male Mbuna. So you have to keep that in mind.

Another difference is in their anal fins. Males will have a sharp pointed anal fin while females will have a more rounded one. Males will also display egg spots on their anal fins, to attract females. But some females can also show these same egg spots.

So you see these identifiers can be misleading. Even to a breeder or your local fish store guy. So use these as kind of an educated guess if you're at the fish store and are about to buy something.

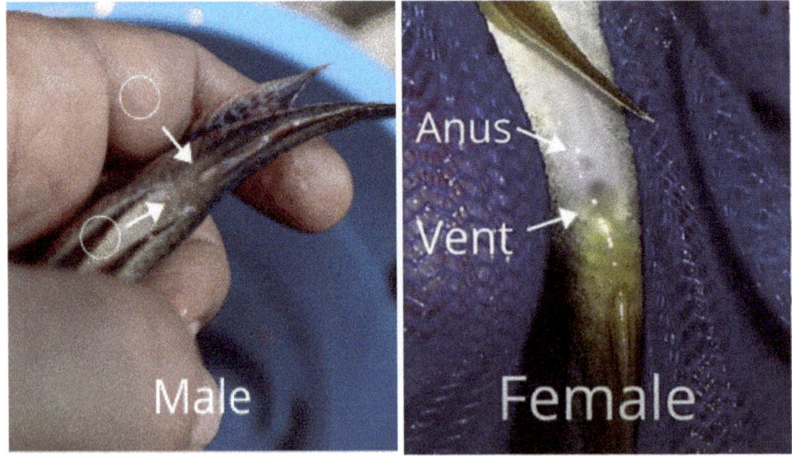

But once you own them and can handle them, venting them will tell you what sex they are.

Venting a fish is when you flip them over and look at their genitals. Males will have 2 identical-sized holes. One hole is their male organ, and the other hole is their anus, where they poop from.

Females will have 2 different-sized holes. The bigger hole is where they lay their eggs and the smaller hole is their anus. One thing to keep in mind is that you can't really vent young fish. They need time to grow and develop these organs to be able to properly tell by venting. Normally you want the fish to be about 3-4” and at least a year old.

Notice the 2 holes and as you can see, it's easy to tell the difference in the sizes of the holes. One is much bigger than the other, making this fish a female.

Here's a comparison between males and females. Easy to tell.

Now that you know how to vent your fish, let me just say that you most likely won't be using this technique much. Most breeders and fish stores do get it right when you ask for guaranteed males. But on the off chance that you're kind of suspicious about one of your guys, venting them would be the best way to get confirmation. Or if you realize your fish is holding eggs in HER mouth, ...yeah, that's a female too lol. But we'll get into more detail about that in the next chapter.

In the next lesson we're going to cover a topic we probably all hate to deal with, quarantine and common diseases.

Lesson Outline:

- Eggs spots, fin curves, and coloration are all good indications of sex but it's not 100% accurate

- 2 same-sized holes is a male, 2 different sizes is a female

- Venting is the only 100% way to be sure of sex

KAVEMAN AQUATICS

Lesson 16

DISEASE AND QUARANTINE

Fish disease is something we have to deal with in all aquarium fish. As much as I want to keep this book specifically on African Cichlids, I felt this is an important listen to make sure we all understand.

Diseases in your fish mainly come from your fish being stressed for one reason or another. When your fish are stressed, it weakens their immune system making it much easier for disease to attack them and succeed. So a key weapon against fighting disease is to make sure your fish aren't stressed!

But let's start with something specific to African Cichlids. African Cichlids are very susceptible to Malawi Bloat. Malawi bloat is a disease where your fish's digestive system is clogged up and they can't poop right. It'll swell up their stomachs and look obvious to you. They'll start breathing heavily and just act very lethargic, like not themselves, not swimming around being happy as usual. You're going to be able to tell something's wrong.

The cause for Malawi bloat has not been 100% determined but some reasons are bad water quality. Not keeping up with your maintenance and allowing your nitrates to reach unsafe levels can cause Malawi Bloat. Also the diet you feed fish may not be optimal.

If you keep Mbunas, this is especially true since they are herbivores. If you feed them a high-fat and protein diet, they will get Malawi bloat.

Which is one of those reasons why I suggest not mixing Mbuna with omnivores like Peacocks and Haps. The protein you feed them will also get eaten by the Mbuna and then you'll have to deal with bloat.

But don't think it's just an Mbuna thing. Your Peacocks and Haps can also get Malawi bloat.

So in the unfortunate chance that your fish get Malawi bloat, how do you treat it? Well, that hasn't been 100% discovered either. But there are a few things that have been known to help if you catch it early.

Clean water, obviously right. Remove the fish into a hospital tank and make sure that the water is pristine, meaning water changes every other day! Also, stop feeding or try feeding skinless peas. Peas help in promoting a good poop.

Epsom Salt is also helpful in reducing swelling and alleviating constipation. Basically, it helps them poop. Start with a small dosage of ¼ teaspoon per 10 gallons daily until symptoms have improved.

If you wanted to try medication right off the bat, many use Seachem Metroplex. When medicating, remember to remove any carbon from the tank or the carbon will remove the meds.

Now of course there are many other diseases besides Malawi bloat that all fish can get but going through each one and its symptoms and causes and treatments...well that would be an entire course in itself.

But the purpose of this lesson is to understand that fish disease is not uncommon. You will have to deal with it at some point and time. This leads me to the next topic of this lesson which is quarantine.

Again, quarantining your fish is a very general subject in the aquarium hobby. This isn't specific to just African Cichlids but I want to stress the importance of quarantining all new fish.

Since I just said the disease in your fish is very common and likely, hopefully that stuck with you, now knowing that why would you ever put a new fish in your tank with all your other healthy guys and take the risk of infecting your whole tank. I wouldn't, and you shouldn't either.

I believe in quarantine more than I can stress. When you build up your tank full of your beautiful choices of fish and you have your favorites and you get attached to them and you love seeing them grow and recognize you and you learn their personalities...I can even tell when one of my guys is in a grumpy mood lol Anyway, my point is, you add in that 1 new fish, or fishes, and all of a sudden, a fish dies, and then another, and then another. Trust me when I tell you, it's a devastating thing to have to go through!

At first, you won't know why the first couple died. Then if more die, you'll be sure it's some kind of disease, but what is it? How do you treat it, what do you do? Believe me when I tell you I've heard stories of people losing an entire tank! I wouldn't wish that on my worst enemies.

Avoid this from happening by just quarantining your new fish for 2 weeks tops! You don't automatically have to treat them if you don't want to. Keep an eye on them, observe, make sure they're eating well and be social with the other fish. If they seem funny, something might be wrong and then you can go ahead and treat them with general meds to cover all the basics.

Or you could just treat right off the bat. In my case if I get a big batch of new fish...say 5-10, I put them all in quarantine and treat the entire tank with what I call "The Quarantine Couple". Seachem ParaGuard and MetroPlex will cover most of the most common diseases. These are very mild medications and will treat parasitic, fungal, and bacterial infections without harming your bio-filter.

I know what it feels like to get new fish and want to add them with your guys right away, but the peace of mind you'll get knowing they aren't bringing any disease to your tank is unmeasurable!

So let me try to make it a bit easier for you to want to keep a quarantine tank...ready....you don't have to keep one! Nope, not at all. Nobody wants to set up an empty tank and keep a filter on it and heater and make sure it's clean all while maybe not getting any new fish for a while, right? Well, you don't have to do that.

The trick is to have an empty 10-20 gallon tank stored away somewhere, and keep a sponge filter in your main tank.

Now when the time comes that you decided to get some new fish, you pop that empty tank out of the closet or out of the garage. Fill it up with DECHLORINATED water! Throw a small heater in there and take your seeded sponge filter out of your main tank and drop it in the quarantine. Now you have a fully cycled quarantine tank ready for those new fish on day 1!

The bacteria that has already grown on your sponge filter while in the main tank will quickly convert any ammonia in your quarantine tank.

Then after your 2-3 week quarantine, yea I know I upped it a week lol, you can simply put your sponge filter back in your main tank and break it down and store away that quarantine tank once again.

And don't worry, you may be thinking about your sponge filter being contaminated with disease. Well, if your fish did have some kind of disease and you did medicate the tank, I'm sure you left that fish in quarantine until there were no signs of disease anymore. So not only did the meds kill the parasites and/or fungus in and on your fish, they did the same on your sponge filter.

Alternatively, if you don't like the look of a sponge filter in your main tank, you can accomplish the same quick quarantine tank setup by removing some bio media from inside your main tank's filter and placing that seeded bio media in the quarantine tanks filter, possible a small hang on back filter.

This completes the chapter on your fish's care and health! And in the next and final chapter, I'm going to give you some specific gems that I feel all African Cichlid keepers should know.

Lesson Outline:

- Diseases is always in your tank. Keep your fish stress free to keep their immune systems healthy

- Clean Water is one of the best medications

- Auto medicate with the QC – Seachem ParaGuard and MetroPlex

- Always quarantine new fish

- You don't have to keep a quarantine tank up and running at all times

Chapter 5

Extras

KAVEMAN AQUATICS

Lesson 17

ADDING NEW AFRICAN CICHLIDS TO THE TANK

I want to give you some extra golden nuggets that can only be learned with time and experience when keeping these fish. Or from a book like this. I'm so happy you decided to purchase it, I hope it's been helpful so far! The lessons in this chapter will provide some extra value for you. Let's get into it!

Adding new fish to your African Cichlid tank is not as simple as you may think it is. Remember, in an African Cichlid tank they have a hierarchy. And fish are in their position in that hierarchy for a reason. So what do you think will happen when new fish enter the tank without a position...that's right, they will sort each other out and the results may not be optimal.

The first thing to understand is that you never add a new fish by itself to an established African Cichlid tank. That one new fish, without a position in the ranking order, will be terrorized, even to the point of possible death.

If you think about it, it makes sense. Every fish in your established tank has a position and it wants to keep its position. Even the guy at the bottom of the totem pole wants someone else to be at the bottom. So nearly every fish you currently have is going to bully and harass that one new fish to let him know that hey, "I'm above you in this ranking order, and you are below me" But if every fish is doing that to the same single fish, that will be super stressful and we know stress is the last thing we want for our fish. That level of stress can easily kill a new lonely fish.

So how do we do it, how do we add new fish? Glad you asked.

You always want to add about 3-5 new fish at the same time. And preferably of a similar size to your current stock. What does that do, well your current fish are still going to act the same way. Attacking, chasing, and harassing the new 3-5 fish, but at least that aggression is mitigated and dissipated from just 1 fish getting the brunt of it. This creates a smaller amount of stress for each individual fish instead of just 1 guy getting the max amount of stress.

Another great tactic is to add your new 3-5 fish during a water change. A water change will distract your fish your current stock. Since they'll be busy dealing with their own current distraction, they may not be too concerned with these new guys you just added.

Also, it would be a good time to move some décor around during the water change. This will reset any territories that your fish may be claiming and defending as their own. Now that you've reset them, they'll be busy trying to reclaim new territory rather than being too concerned with the new guys. Keeping the lights off after adding in new guys can help in reducing some stress as well.

Now there may be a situation when you've only got 1 fish to add. Maybe you saw an absolute stud in the fish store while you were on your occasional window-shopping trips. That you swore to yourself you weren't gonna buy any fish and then....yea, I know, don't worry, no judgment, we've all been there lol.

Or maybe you had a sick fish in a hospital tank that you were medicating and now he's all better and ready to go back in the main tank, what do you do? Excellent question. I've got the trick for you, here's what you do!

You add fish from your main tank in with your new guy....ah, let me explain.

If it's a new fish, I hope you quarantine that new fish like we just discussed in the previous lesson, or if it's your old guy that has just gotten better in your hospital tank, either way, we have 1 fish ready to go into the main tank. At this point what you can do is choose any 2-4 fish from your main and add them to your quarantine/hospital with the 1 fish.

There will be little to no aggression in the quarantine tank because everyone is new there, basically. Everyone is confused and wondering what's going on. Nobody has any territory, not even the 1 fish that was in there alone because he didn't have to defend anything from anyone, so aggression will stay at a minimum in there.

Leave them together for about a week or so, so the hierarchy in your main tank can reset or adjust accordingly and then introduce all the fish from quarantine into the main tank together using all of the previous tactics already discussed and they'll be good to go. Cool right!

In the next lesson, we'll discuss breeding in African Cichlids, how it happens, what it entails, and what to do if you end up with a bunch of fry.

Lesson Outline:

- Never add only 1 new African Cichlid to an established tank

- Always add about 3-5 fish together

- Adding during a water change can help as a distraction

- Lights off after adding new fish can help mitigate stress

Lesson 18

BREEDING

Even though most of you are not getting into these fish for breeding purposes, it may happen unexpectedly in your tank and I want you to be equipped with the basic information so you know what to do.

Breeding African Cichlids can be fun and fulfilling for a hobbyist, watching them grow from a tiny egg and waiting for the surprise of what kind of colors might emerge is super cool. But breeding can be a daunting task for the average fish keeper. You'll need more tanks, more equipment, and you'll need a lot of patience for sure.

I'm not going to make this the huge topic that it is because I'm going to assume the majority of you aren't going to get into that right away in your new African Cichlid journey. But we will cover the basics of what you should know about your fish.

African Cichlids are mouth brooders, which means that the female lays eggs and when they are fertilized by the male, they scoop them into their mouths and incubate them there for about 3 weeks to a month. During this incubation period, the female will not eat and mostly stay to herself in a corner or a favorite hiding spot. You will also be able to tell that she's holding because her mouth will look bigger, wider, and fuller as she makes room for what could be 50 eggs at a time. After the fry grow into free swimmers, she will spit them out, leaving them to survive in the wild on their own.

But let's take a step back, how does this happen in the first place? When you've got males and females in the same tank, with optimal water conditions, they will mate, a lot! The dominant male will be the brightest and the most confident. He'll dig out a cave or a hole in the substrate and lure the female into it, while also chasing all other males away from his special place. When the male and the female engage, they'll begin a sort of dance ritual which will look like them spinning around each other in a circle. The male will also shake and vibrate and spread his fins showing his masterful self.

What's happening is the female is spitting out eggs while the male fertilizes them and then she scoops them up. This dance ritual can take hours if the female has a lot of eggs to lay. Every time an intruder comes into the dance, the male will chase them away and then the dance resets. When you see this for the first time in your tank, you'll know exactly what it looks like.

Now if you're keeping an all-male tank as I suggested early, this dance shouldn't happen at all right? Wrong. Sometimes two males will get into this very similar dance pattern but what it is, is a show of dominance. Which male is dominant over the other? Sometimes it ends with who has the better show of it, but sometimes it can be the beginning of a big fight. So keep an eye out for it in your all-male tanks as well.

What do you do if you realize you've got a female holding eggs in your tank? Well, it depends on what you want to do at this point. If you just want to have your one main African Cichlid tank display, then you don't have to do anything. She will eventually spit them out and the strongest will survive. Which is a nice way of saying many of them will get eaten. But that's the circle of life.

Now if you did want to keep the fry and raise them, then there's a whole procedure for that. To keep it simple, what you will need is a separate quarantine/holding tank for the female and a grow-out tank. You could remove the female and move her to the holding tank and wait for her to spit out the fry there, but this can take a while. And remember, she won't be eating this whole time. So what most people do is "strip" her of the eggs.

You can do this by gently opening her mouth until all the eggs fall out. The eggs should go in what's called a "tumbler" to keep the eggs moving and active as the fry grow. When the fry completely lose their egg sack, you can then move them to a fry tank or a grow-out tank where they'll remain there until they're big enough to either be sold if that's what you wanted to do or big enough to join your main tank with the big boys.

Now I want to remind you about being patient. The process from eggs to big enough to leave the grow out could take 6 months to a year, and they'll still be pretty small at that point. But like I said, if you wanted to expand your hobby into breeding and raising fry, it can be very rewarding, but it won't be a cakewalk either.

In the next lesson, we'll discuss what to expect in the long term while keeping African Cichlids, what happens as they grow and multiply, and what could potentially happen to you as a hobbyist.

Lesson Outline:

- African Cichlids are mouth brooders

- Females will hold for about 3 weeks

- Stripping eggs is not required but can allow the female to eat again

- Stripped eggs must go into an egg tumbler

Lesson 19

WHAT TO EXPECT AS THEY GROW

ALL RIGHT!! Now that you've got a good grasp on how to keep a successful African Cichlid tank, let's talk about some of the things you can expect as your fish grow.

Since we just covered all that comes with keeping and raising fry, for this lesson we'll discuss starting with juveniles and we'll work our way up to adults. But of course, you don't have to start with juveniles, you can always start with full-grown adult fish as well if you like.

Normally you would want to keep juveniles in a grow-out tank. Something like a 40 gallon long, or a 55 gallon while they grow and get ready for your main tank with your bigger fish. But if you're just starting with African Cichlids, I'm sure that your grow-out tank will also be your main tank, lol so let's start there.

Your juveniles are going to grow quickly. Especially since you should be feeding them between 2-3 times a day. But still making sure they consume all the food in under a minute. You can expect to see a difference in their size almost daily, a very small difference, but you'll notice.

They'll sort out the hierarchy fairly quickly and you'll begin to notice which fish are more dominant than others. Both because they'll begin to show color before any others but also because they'll be the ones doing the chasing, and not getting chased.

When starting with juveniles, it's also very likely that you may end up with some females. This is common because some fish aren't developed enough yet when they're that young and small. This is another good reason for the grow-out tank, as they grow and develop and start showing more gender signs you can separate females from males before adding them into your main tank and creating problems.

Let me tell you about a very common way that we "fish-keeping-lovers" end up with MTS, which stands for multiple tank syndrome. One way is the need for grow-out tanks.

As your juveniles grow closer to full adult size which can be anywhere from 5" to 12" or more, during that time you may have been adding more fish to your tank here and there, finding a rare stud in the store and thinking, I must have that guy! Don't worry, it happens. Well now that your guys have grown and gotten bigger, you'll begin to wonder if the 55-gallon tank you started with just isn't big enough for them anymore. It happens, trust me, I'm trying to get you prepared for the inevitable.

So you think it over, you look at your budget, you check the available space in your place and you ultimately decide to upgrade your tank. Ok, all well and good, pretty normal thing in the hobby. Now you may have been thinking about selling your old tank because you don't need it anymore, right...wrong! You may quickly realize that buying big full-grown fish can get pretty expensive, and it's more economical to buy juveniles. Not only that but you enjoyed watching them grow and blossom into the big beautiful fish they are now, but by this point you know you can't keep new juvenile fish with your bigger adult fish in their big new upgraded tank......and then, your grow out tank is born!

Your old tank becomes your grow-out, now you have 2 tanks instead of 1 and you're on your way to being diagnosed with MTS! No judgment, it happens to the best of us.

Now you've got big adult fish in your main tank, what can you expect? If you've kept them altogether since juveniles, they have worked out the hierarchy long ago and if you followed all the suggestions earlier on in the book about dealing with aggression, your tank should be calm and cool by now. But let's say you started with adults.

In this case, you're going to need to keep a close eye on who is leading the school. Sometimes you can get a good tank boss that keeps everyone in their place, but without harming other fish, or you can get a bad tank boss that wants to kill anyone that comes near his self-proclaimed territory. If you spot a bully like this in your tank, you will want to remove him quickly. The longer he stays in the tank, the more submissive your other fish will get which can stunt their growth, keep them stressed, and even make their colors look dim and pale.

Now when I say "a bully" I don't mean the occasional chase here and there. That is always going to happen from fish to fish in an African Cichlid tank. It's their way of reiterating their position in the hierarchy to the less dominant fish. Totally normal. When I say a bully, I mean the fish that won't stop chasing a fish until they catch him and inflict damage on him. That should not be tolerated in your tank at all and that bully must be removed. You can try the time-out method we discussed earlier, but remember that has just a 50/50 success rate. So be prepared to possibly have to rehome a fish like that. And guess what, usually the bullies are the biggest, brightest, and prettiest of them all...nature of the species.

In the next and final lesson, it's time to get practical, time to take action!

Chapter 6

Time to take action!

KAVEMAN AQUATICS

You made it! Congratulations! You are on your way to starting your African Cichlid tank or to improving the quality of the African Cichlid tank you already have. Bravo!

It's time to kick-start your journey by providing you with some practical information to get you going right now!

First, I want you to check out a free app that I still use to this day. I don't own this app and I'm not affiliated with it in any way, it's just a great tool! It's called "the fish companion" and it will help you to identify different species of African Cichlids from all three groups, Peacocks, Haps, and Mbuna. Search your app store for "the fish companion"

Unfortunately, some people have told me it's not available in their app store anymore, if that's the case for you then go directly to their website at fishcompanion.com

Next, I want to share with you all of the best online fish breeders that I use myself, including discount codes! But before you place any orders, make sure your tank is up and running, and cycled beforehand as these guys ship overnight!

The first one is my buddy Neil over at CoastalCichlids.com He has quality fish and excellent service! Use code kaveman10 for a 10% discount and if you speak to Neil directly, tell'm the Kaveman sent you haha.

The next best spot is imperialtropicals.com. Again, excellent fish, shipping, and service. I have never had a problem with them. Use code KAVEMAN for a 5% discount on your order.

And last but not least is SnakeRiverCichlids.com. They've got some amazing OBs with awesome color patterns like you've never seen. Use code kaveman2022 for a 15% discount on your order.

Side Note. These suppliers and discount codes may change or be updated after the printing of this book. To make sure you have the latest discount codes they will always be updated in my Facebook Group. The group is also a great place to find like-minded fish keepers helping each other and sharing their journey and experiences, a community of hobbyist's just like you. 😊 Visit:

– Facebook.com/groups/KaveManAquatics

And finally, I've put together a very convenient one-stop shop for all the aquarium products and equipment discussed in this book. You can find it on my website under the shop tab or you can go directly to KaveManAquatics.com/Shop

The links to most products are amazon affiliate links which means I will get a small commision from the products you purchase at no extra cost to you. So I appreciate you using my links. Those commissions directly help to grow the brand and the community!

Congratulation! You are on your way to becoming an expert African Cichlid keeper! I hope you found great value in this book. I poured my heart and soul into it to make sure you could feel confident about keeping your own African Cichlids, and please, please, share your tanks with me and the community! If you're not part of the Facebook group already you can join us at Facebook.com/Groups/KaveManAquatics and post your pictures of your new beautiful African Cichlid tank there.

Lastly, your feedback means everything to me! Please let me know if you enjoyed the book and found it helpful in your fish keeping journey! I really hope so!

Leave your review at KaveManAquatics.com/Shop

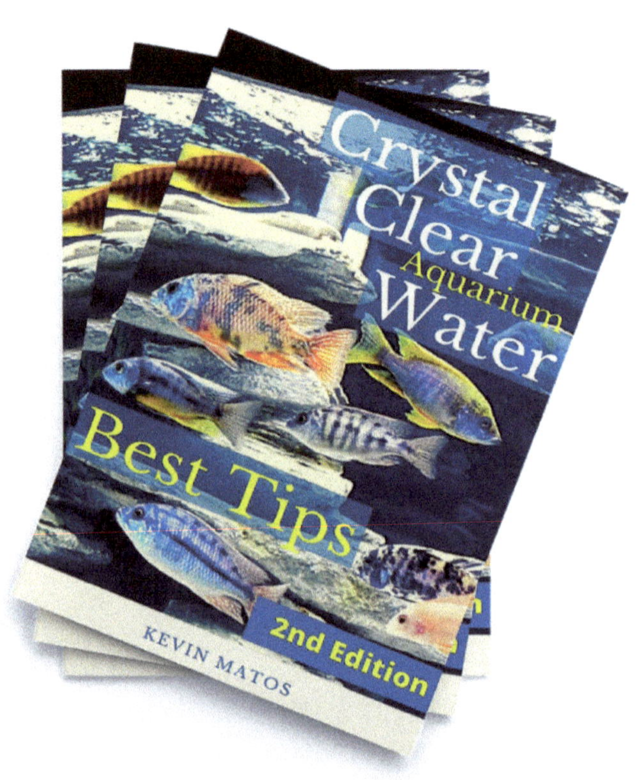

KaveManAquatics.com/Crystal-Clear-Aquarium-Water-eBook

KaveManAquatics.com/African-Cichlids-Course

Index

A

acidic water, 23
aggression, 6–7, 9–10, 12, 17–19, 21, 32, 39, 51, 55, 88–89, 97
aggression problems, 19, 63
air pumps, battery-operated, 56
algae, 18, 22, 26
alkaline, 46, 73
alkaline water, 25–26
amino acids, 64
aragonite sand, 47–49, 71–72

B

breeders, best online fish, 101
breeding, 19, 89, 91, 93
buffer, 47, 71–72
buffering capacity, 47–48
bully, 11–12, 18, 87, 97

C

caves, 10, 18, 92
Cichlid Lake Salt, 48, 73
Cichlid Salt and Malawi buffer, 71–72
Cichlid Trace, 73
clown loaches, 21–24
coloration, 64, 77
colors, 14, 21, 61, 67, 75, 91, 96–97
crushed coral, 47–49, 71–72
crushed coral and aragonite sand, 47–48
cycle, nitrogen, 57, 69

D

dechlorinate, 73–74
décor, 10, 13–14, 18, 22, 32, 71, 88
diet, 13–14, 18, 61, 67, 79
diseases, 10, 63, 67, 70, 79–83

E

eggs, 76–77, 91–93
eggs spots, 75, 77
Epsom Salt, 80

F

Facebook Group, 102
feeding, 14, 51, 61, 63, 66–67, 95
feeding frequency, 65
feeding pellets, 64–66
feeding regiment, mixed, 14
female African Cichlids, 74
females, 7, 11, 14, 17, 19, 75–76, 93, 96
female-to-male ratio, high, 19
filter, 34–35, 37, 47, 66, 82–83
  canister, 36
  main tank's, 83
  quarantine tanks, 83
filter intake, 22, 40
filtration, 21, 27, 35
fish
  aggressive, 10
  dominant, 6, 14, 97
fish color, 64, 67
flakes, 62
flow rate, 36–37
food, 62–64, 66–67, 95
  uneaten, 40, 71
fry, 19, 89, 92–93
  raising, 93, 95

G

GarlicGuard, 63–64

H

haps, 6, 13–15, 17, 21, 62, 67, 75, 80, 101
heater, 41, 51–53, 82